Pocahontas

by Lola M. Schaefer

Consulting Editor: Gail Saunders-Smith, Ph.D.
Consultant: Melodie Andrews, Ph.D.
Associate Professor of Early American History
Minnesota State University, Mankato

Pebble Books

an imprint of Capstone Press
Mankato, Minnesota

Pebble Books are published by Capstone Press
151 Good Counsel Drive, P.O. Box 669, Mankato, Minnesota 56002
www.capstonepress.com

2 3 4 5 6 07 06 05 04 03 02

Library of Congress Cataloging-in-Publication Data
Schaefer, Lola M., 1950–
    Pocahontas / by Lola M. Schaefer.
    p. cm.—(First biographies)
    Includes bibliographical references (p. 23) and index.
    Summary: Simple text and illustrations introduce the life of the Powhatan
Indian who worked throughout her life to establish peace between her people and
the English.
    ISBN-13: 978-0-7368-1175-0 (hardcover)
    ISBN-10: 0-7368-1175-3 (hardcover)
    ISBN-13: 978-0-7368-9372-5 (softcover pbk.)
    ISBN-10: 0-7368-9372-5 (softcover pbk.)
    1. Pocahontas, d. 1617—Juvenile literature. 2. Powhatan women—Biography—
Juvenile literature. 3. Powhatan Indians—History—Juvenile literature. 4. Smith,
John, 1580-1631—Juvenile literature. 5. Jamestown (Va.)—History—Juvenile
literature. [1. Pocahontas, d. 1617. 2. Powhatan Indians—Biography. 3. Indians of
North America—Virginia—Biography. 4. Jamestown (Va.)—History.] I. Title.
II. Series: First biographies (Mankato, Minn.)
E99.P85 P5785 2002
975.5′01′092—dc21   2001004834

Note to Parents and Teachers

The First Biographies series supports national history standards for units
on people and culture. This book describes and illustrates the life of
Pocahontas. The photographs support early readers in understanding the
text. This book also introduces early readers to subject-specific vocabulary
words, which are defined in the Words to Know section. Early readers may
need assistance to read some words and to use the Table of Contents,
Words to Know, Read More, Internet Sites, and Index/Word List sections of
the book.

Table of Contents

Time Line

around 1595
Pocahontas is born.

Pocahontas was born in America around 1595. She and her family were Native Americans. Her father was Chief Powhatan. She was his favorite daughter. He listened to her ideas.

Pocahontas statue in Jamestown, Virginia

Time Line

around 1595
Pocahontas is born.

1607
First English
settlers arrive.

In 1607, English settlers came to America. They built Jamestown on land ruled by Chief Powhatan. Captain John Smith was the leader of Jamestown.

English settlers building Jamestown

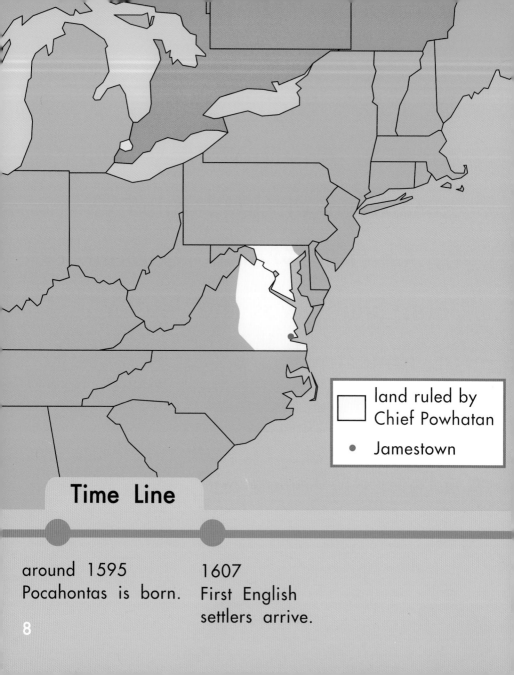

land ruled by
Chief Powhatan

• Jamestown

Time Line

around 1595
Pocahontas is born.

1607
First English
settlers arrive.

8

The Native Americans and the settlers traded food and tools. The Native Americans were willing to share their land. But the settlers wanted to own the land. Fighting soon began.

Time Line

around 1595
Pocahontas is born.

1607
First English
settlers arrive.

1609
Captain Smith
returns to England.

Pocahontas and her people wanted peace. Pocahontas helped make peace with the settlers. But fighting began again when Captain Smith returned to England in 1609.

peaceful trade between settlers and Native Americans

Time Line

around 1595
Pocahontas is born.

1607
First English
settlers arrive.

1609
Captain Smith
returns to England.

The settlers captured Pocahontas. They kept her at Jamestown for one year. Chief Powhatan missed his daughter. The settlers talked with Chief Powhatan about returning Pocahontas.

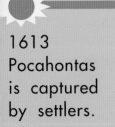

1613
Pocahontas
is captured
by settlers.

Time Line

around 1595
Pocahontas is born.

1607
First English
settlers arrive.

1609
Captain Smith
returns to England.

14

The settlers dressed
Pocahontas in English
clothes. They taught her how
to write and speak English.
Pocahontas wanted to teach
the settlers about her people.

◀ Pocahontas dressed as an Englishwoman

1613
Pocahontas
is captured
by settlers.

Time Line

around 1595	1607	1609
Pocahontas is born.	First English settlers arrive.	Captain Smith returns to England.

In 1614, Pocahontas married an Englishman named John Rolfe. They had a son named Thomas. Pocahontas, John, and Thomas went on a trip to England.

◀ marriage of Pocahontas and John Rolfe

1613	1614	1616
Pocahontas is captured by settlers.	Pocahontas marries John Rolfe.	Pocahontas travels to England.

Time Line

around 1595
Pocahontas is born.

1607
First English
settlers arrive.

1609
Captain Smith
returns to England.

Pocahontas spoke with the king and queen of England. She wanted the English to respect Native Americans. She wanted the settlers and Native Americans to live together peacefully.

1613
Pocahontas is captured by settlers.

1614
Pocahontas marries John Rolfe.

1616
Pocahontas travels to England.

Time Line

around 1595
Pocahontas is born.

1607
First English
settlers arrive.

1609
Captain Smith
returns to England.

Pocahontas died in England in 1617. She wanted Native Americans and the English to understand each other. She worked hard for peace.

1613
Pocahontas
is captured
by settlers.

1614
Pocahontas
marries
John Rolfe.

1616
Pocahontas
travels to
England.

1617
Pocahontas
dies.

Words to Know

capture—to take a person or a place by force

chief—the leader of a group of people

England—a country in Western Europe; England is now part of the United Kingdom.

leader—someone who leads a group of people

Native American—a person related to the first people who lived in North or South America

respect—to admire and have a high opinion of someone; respect means to treat others the way you would like to be treated.

settler—a person who makes a home in a new place

trade—to exchange one item for another; the Native Americans traded corn and fish to the English settlers in exchange for beads and bells.

Read More

Hudson, Margaret. *Pocahontas.* Lives and Times. Des Plaines, Ill.: Heinemann Interactive Library, 1999.

Jenner, Caryn. *The Story of Pocahontas.* New York: Dorling Kindersley, 2000.

Shaughnessy, Diane. *Pocahontas: Powhatan Princess.* Famous Native Americans. New York: PowerKids Press, 1997.

Internet Sites

Pocahontas
http://school.discovery.com/homeworkhelp/worldbook/atozhistory/p/435960.html

Pocahontas
http://www.incwell.com/Biographies/Pocahontas.html

The Pocahontas Myth
http://www.powhatan.org/pocc.html

Virtual Jamestown: Pocahontas
http://jefferson.village.virginia.edu/vcdh/jamestown/Pocahontas.html

Index/Word List

America, 5
captured, 13
clothes, 15
daughter,
  5, 13
England, 11,
  17, 19, 21
fighting, 9, 11
food, 9
Jamestown,
  7, 13
land, 7, 9
leader, 7
married, 17

Native
  Americans,
  5, 9, 19, 21
peace, 11, 21
peacefully, 19
people, 11, 15
Powhatan,
  Chief
  (father), 5,
  7, 13
respect, 19
Rolfe, John
  (husband),
  17

Rolfe, Thomas
  (son), 17
settlers, 7, 9,
  13, 15, 19
Smith, Captain
  John, 7, 11
son, 17
teach, 15
together, 19
trade, 9, 11
trip, 17
understand,
  21
write, 15

Word Count: 234
Early-Intervention Level: 24

Editorial Credits

Martha E. H. Rustad, editor; Heather Kindseth, cover designer and illustrator;
    Linda Clavel, illustrator; Kimberly Danger, Mary Englar, and Jo Miller,
    photo researchers

Photo Credits

HultonGetty/Archive Photos, cover
National Park Service/Colonial National Historic Park, 6
North Wind Picture Archives, 4, 10, 12, 16, 18, 20
Stock Montage, Inc., 1, 14